The History of Ru

BY

Stephan Weaver

© 2015 Copyright

No part of this book may be reproduced in any form or by any electronic or mechanical means including information storage and retrieval systems, without permission in writing from the author.

TABLE OF CONTENTS

Prehistoric Russia

The Stone Age—2.5 million-3000 BC

The Earlier Tribes of Russia—1500BC-900AD

Slav Rule—1500 BC

Cimmerian Rule –1200 BC

Scythian Rule –300 BC

Goth Rule–270 AD

Hun Rule—375 AD

Khazar Rule—576-965 AD

ESSEX COUNTY
COUNCIL LIBRARY

Viking Russia

Rurik Becomes Prince of Novogard—860 AD

Oleg Founded Kievan Rus'—882 AD

Vladimir I—980-1015

Vladimir I Adapts Greek Orthodoxy—988 AD

Medieval Russia

The Erosion of Kievan Rus'—(11th century)

The Invasion of the Mongols (Tatar Rule)—1223-1240

The Emergence of Muscovy—1283

Ivan III Vasilyevich (Ivan the Great)—1462-1505

Ivan Destroys Novgorod—1478

Russia's Tsars

Ivan IV (Ivan the Terrible) Becomes the First Tsar— 1547

Livonian War—1558-1583

Boris Godunov Becomes a Boyar— 1584

The Three False Dmitrys— 1604-1613

Peter the Great Becomes a Tsar— 1682-1725

Massive Transformation Under the Rule of Peter I—1703

Tsarevich Alexis Flees Russia—1716

Seventy Years of Empresses

Catherine I Becomes Empress— 1724

Anna Builds a Court Composed of Foreigners and Upsets Russians— 1730

Elizabeth Organizes a Coup— 1741

Catherine the Great Becomes Empress— 1762-1796

The Early 19th Century Russia

Alexander I Become a Tsar—1801

Napoleon Invades Russia— 1812

Nicholas I—1825

The Crimean War— 1853-56

Russia Sells Alaska to America— 1867

The Revolutionary Era of Russia

The new Tsar Nicholas II—1894

The establishment of the Russian Social Democratic Labor Party –1898

War With Japan— 1904

Conclusion of the Russo-Japanese War – 1905

Bloody Sunday— 1905

The Signing of the October Manifesto— 1905

Early 20th Century Russia

Russia in World War I— 1914

The February Revolution – 1917

The End of the Tsar Era—1917

The October Revolution – 1917

The Civil War—1918

Modern Russia

The Formation of the Soviet Union— 1922

The World War II—1939-1945

The Cold War 1945-1990

The Soviet Union Collapses—1991

Russia Becomes a Member of the BRICS—2009

The Ukrainian Conflict and Russia's Annexation of Crimea—2014-2015

Introduction

Russia's hypnotic steppe is not just a bounty of nature, but also the major appeal to the many migrants that crossed its boarders to start a life. This spellbinding land has hosted the rise and fall of many kingdoms, hailing from distant parts of the world such as Mongolia, Scandinavia, and Turkey.

This eBook runs through 50 of the most riveting accounts of Russian history. From prehistoric to modern Russia, each epoch that gave rise to the many entrancing features of Russia is discussed.

Goth Rule, Kievan Rus, Viking Russia, Tsar Rule, Socialist Russia—there is no part of this nation's history that is left out.

Prehistoric Russia

Much like any other country of prehistoric times, Russia was the site of migrating nomads and ancient kingdoms. Since the 2nd millennium B.C., prehistoric Russia has hosted the coming and going of a legion of peoples; each of them took turns in imprinting their culture and dominant traits. Perhaps the migration was mostly facilitated by the steppe.

An assimilation of tribes ranging from Mongolians to Germanic tribes spread throughout Russia.

2.5 million-3000 B.C.

The Stone Age

Archeological discoveries, notably the exhumation of the 1,500,000 year old flint tools of Oldwans in Caucasus, show the existence of early humans in Russia. Further finds of archeology show that some of the last surviving groups of Neanderthals lived in Russia. A skeleton of a Neanderthal child was found in Adygea, located between southwestern Russia and northwestern Caucasus. According to the carbon dating, the skeleton is 29,000 years old.

The male Oldwans were hunters and the female were gatherers who looked after their children. They crafted simple tools like knives and hammers from stones. They had social groups that hunted and gathered together.

The steppe had a climate conducive to plant life, but one that was not sufficient to support sedentary farming; therefore, the inhabitants of the area—inherently herders from the start—would remain long enough for their cattle to finish grazing on the grass in the area. They would then simply migrate elsewhere.

In Russia, the steppe located in today's Ukraine was also a prominent factor in the movement. Named after the ancient title of the Black Sea, Pontus Euxinus, this section of the grassland is sometimes referred to as the Pontic-Caspian Steppe (also known as Scythia in classical antiquity). Stretching extensively and uninterruptedly from Mongolia to Hungary, the Pontic-Caspian Steppe bestowed an immaculate path for the travel of nomads and their cattle. The majority of these nomads are believed to have hailed from Mongolia. They often followed the steppe all the way to Europe, Middle East or India.

1500 BC-900 A.D.

The Earlier Tribes of Russia

For over a millennium, the steppes saw the rise and fall of several kingdoms. The Scythians, Cimmerians, Goths, Huns, Avars and Khazars were but a few.

Little is known about the inhabitants of Russia in the prehistoric era. As these dwellers were illiterate, the rags of evidence were collected from the bordering civilizations: from the west, Assyria (modern day northern Iraq) and Greek; from the east, China. Certain artifacts of the era are also used as the foundations of evidence.

Researches show that they were nomadic herders whose diets consisted of dairy products and meat. Archeological findings also show that the dwellers domesticated horses as early as the third millennium B.C., perhaps even earlier than that.

Generally, however, the ancestors of today's Russia can be dissected into four tribes: Turkish tribes; Mongolic tribes; Indo-Europeans, namely the Slavs and the Balts (these tribes are believed to constitute the majority of Russians; they are believed to have hailed from parts of the Middle East); and Finns (Finno-Ugric tribes).

Slav Rule

The fist rulers of the steppes are believed to be of Indo-European origin, namely the Slavs. They settled in the regions of western Russia and Poland in 1500 B.C. Precious little evidence exists of the presence of the early Slavs; most of what is known about them today is sourced from the hearsay of the neighboring Germanic tribes.

They were known by the Romans as "Venedi", but they only had a close acquaintance with the Slavs when the Germanic tribes captured and sold them as slaves. Although the name Slav means "glorious", the inundation of Slavs sold to slavery at the time led to the English meaning "slave".

Poor, ill-organized and weak, the Slavs were overran and exploited by a legion of tribes that settled in the steppes for the centuries to come (the 4th century to the 9th century). Sure, they were no match for the wave of valiant warriors that terrorized them, but the Slavs were unmatched in the battle of procreation. The race of the Slavs multiplied, outnumbering their bellicose invaders.

As the population grew, the Slavs sprawled in seek of new land to settle on. They went west to the Elbe Rivers, east until reaching the dominions of the Khazars and the Volga Bulgars, south to the Balkans and north to the Finns.

Kingdoms came and went but the Slavs remained a silent yet dominant presence holding on to most of their territories until the arrival of the Vikings.

1200 B.C.

Cimmerian Rule

Cimmerians are believed to have settled north of the Black Sea as early as 1200 B.C. Sources from Greece and Assyria help support the belief. Herodotus, the Greek Historian, in his literary work Odyssey, states that these tribes dwelt in the gateways of Hades. He further states that they were ousted by the Scythians.

The earliest mention of Cimmerians in Assyria is by King Sargon II (722-705 B.C.). In depicting his battle with Urartu (a sovereignty situated in today's Armenia), he mentions the help of the Gimirri (meaning "the people traveling back and forth"). Gimirri is another term for Cimmerians.

300 B.C.

Scythian Rule

After expelling the Cimmerians, the Scythians maintained dominion over large tracts of the steppe. However, after 350 B.C. they were in turn expelled by other Indo-European expansions such as that of the Macedonians under Philip of Macedon, the Celts and the Samaritans.

The Scythians were Indo-Iranian nomads accredited for instituting the horse-based lifestyle in prehistoric Russia. The graves of Scythians exhumed from parts of Russia and Serbia in the 18th century show exquisite gold jewelries with carves of the most realistic portraits of animals and humans.

Scythians were war-mongers who played crucial roles in the emergence and fall of bordering kingdoms such as the Assyrian kingdom. But they weren't all together bellicose as they maintained a settled life, embracing the animals that secured their survival, and traded on the black sea coast with the colonies of Greece.

270 A.D.

Goth Rule

Following the rule of the Samaritans and the Cimmerians Bosporus, the Goths of Germanic tribes entered the Black Sea. They arrived in 230 A.D. and unlike their predecessors of migrants, these clans travelled westwards to the steppes rather than eastwards.

In the wake of their arrival (250-260 A.D.) the Goths pursued a campaign of ransacking. Asia Minor, Greece and the Bosporan Kingdom were targets of their raids. In 270 A.D., Aurelian the Roman Emperor ceded Dacia/Romania to the Goths after deeming it indefensible. This triumph led to the split of the Goths into three tribes: Visigoths, Ostrogoths, and Gepids. The Gepids and Visigoths settled in Dacia, while the Ostrogoths forged ahead to settle in today's Ukraine. Under the Goths, Ukraine was known as 'Oium.'

Ermanaric, one of the greatest rulers of the Ostrogoths whose reign spanned from 342-372 A.D., revolutionized the Ostrogoths tradition of chasing off the bordering habitants, namely the Balts, Samartians and the Slavs. He pursued a strategic policy of expansion, invading these lands and their people. Ermanaric swiftly expanded the kingdom of the Ostrogoths, with the territory extending from the Baltic to the Black Seas (today's Belarus, Poland, Latvia, Ukraine and Lithuania).

This ambitious expansion was not without consequences. The territory of the Ostrogoths stretched all the way to the Volga River banks, bringing the tribe in conflict with the Huns from the east and the Alans from the south.

What sounded the knell for Goth dominance was when Ermanaric challenged the Huns. Balmir (Balamber), the Hun leader, responded with a robust and overwhelming surprise attack. The Goth lancers were no match for the mounted archers of the Huns. They devastated the Ostrogoth kingdom and Ermanaric committed suicide in shock of what had happened. His successor Vithimir (372-376) was of little challenge to the Huns who not only crushed the resistance he and his army put up, but also killed him in the course of the events.

The Hun rule prevailed through Russia, forcing some of the Ostrogoths and Visigoths to seek refuge in the Roman Empire during the last years of the 4th century A.D.

These Goth tribes remained dormant until the fall of the Roman Empire—an event they played a crucial role in.

375 A.D.

Hun Rule

As discussed earlier, the Huns countered the Goth provocation with unremitting attacks, bringing the kingdom to its crumpling dusk. By 375 A.D., the Huns became the new rulers of the western Steppes, with their dominion stretching from the Caspian Sea to the country of Hungary.

Originally from Mongolia, the Huns were seen as preeminent threats by both the Chinese and the Romans. So large was their menacing presence that the Chinese built the Great Wall of China to keep them out. This was following the strong Kingdom the Huns

Ermanaric, one of the greatest rulers of the Ostrogoths whose reign spanned from 342-372 A.D., revolutionized the Ostrogoths tradition of chasing off the bordering habitants, namely the Balts, Samartians and the Slavs. He pursued a strategic policy of expansion, invading these lands and their people. Ermanaric swiftly expanded the kingdom of the Ostrogoths, with the territory extending from the Baltic to the Black Seas (today's Belarus, Poland, Latvia, Ukraine and Lithuania).

This ambitious expansion was not without consequences. The territory of the Ostrogoths stretched all the way to the Volga River banks, bringing the tribe in conflict with the Huns from the east and the Alans from the south.

What sounded the knell for Goth dominance was when Ermanaric challenged the Huns. Balmir (Balamber), the Hun leader, responded with a robust and overwhelming surprise attack. The Goth lancers were no match for the mounted archers of the Huns. They devastated the Ostrogoth kingdom and Ermanaric committed suicide in shock of what had happened. His successor Vithimir (372-376) was of little challenge to the Huns who not only crushed the resistance he and his army put up, but also killed him in the course of the events.

The Hun rule prevailed through Russia, forcing some of the Ostrogoths and Visigoths to seek refuge in the Roman Empire during the last years of the 4th century A.D.

These Goth tribes remained dormant until the fall of the Roman Empire—an event they played a crucial role in.

375 A.D.

Hun Rule

As discussed earlier, the Huns countered the Goth provocation with unremitting attacks, bringing the kingdom to its crumpling dusk. By 375 A.D., the Huns became the new rulers of the western Steppes, with their dominion stretching from the Caspian Sea to the country of Hungary.

Originally from Mongolia, the Huns were seen as preeminent threats by both the Chinese and the Romans. So large was their menacing presence that the Chinese built the Great Wall of China to keep them out. This was following the strong Kingdom the Huns built in 3rd century B.C. Once China became a large force, it conquered Mongolia in the late 1st century A.D., chasing the Huns out of their country of origin and to the steppes near the Caspian Sea.

The Huns were originally of Asiatic descent but as they were pushed westwards by the Chinese they mixed with Caucasian races (mostly the Finns) and became mixed.

Unlike its predecessors, this clan was not too ambitious. They didn't have any policies of expansion, and after crossing over to Europe in 375 A.D., they more or less left the neighboring Romans and Germanic tribes unmolested.

This was the case until 390 A.D., when the tribe took on the massive mission of raiding the regions of Caucasus including Persia, Armenia and the colonies of the Eastern Roman Empire such as Syria and Cappadocia. In 398 A.D., the Roman officer Eutropius amassed a large Roman army of Goth and Roman soldiers and crushed the incursion.

The Hun kingdom continued to erode in the 5th century. The Romans played a crucial rule in their downfall, stimulating tribal fights by paying one group to kill the other. Eventually the Huns receded to the steppes and ceded land that they no longer had power to possess to the Romans. The last remnants of the Ostrogoths in the Crimea reclaimed their independence and sustained the legacy of Ermanaric. This was the setting of prehistoric Russia before the invasion of yet another wave of barbarians: The Turkish Avars.

576-965 A.D.

Khazar Rule

The Khazars ruled following the kingdoms of the Turkish Avars and Volga Bulgars (in truth, the Bulagars were a mixture of local tribes comprising the Huns, Goths, Scythians, Turks and Sarmatians). These Khazars had already arrived in the steppes, but it wasn't until fifty years after their arrival that their presence was felt; nonetheless, during the period of 576-626 A.D., they began to fortify their forces.

The Khazars considered themselves an offshoot of the western Turkish Khanate (modern day Kyrgyzstan).

During the Perso-Roman war, in 626 A.D., the Khazar were called for help by the Roman Emperor Heraclius. They provided around 40,000 of their men in the war. The Khazars then pursued a policy of expansion for which they received help from their counterparts in western Turkey and Heraclius. The tribe managed to conquer Transcaucasia, Derbent (627 A.D.) and Tblisi (628 A.D.).

Their kingdom was threatened shortly after these triumphant conquests. In the periods between 643 A.D. and 652 A.D., the Khazars faced the invasion of the Arab Muslims, but they put up a strong resistance and repelled the conquerors. The decisive event was that of 652 A.D. where the two warring parties met in a fierce battle. About 4,000 Arabs were killed; this led the invaders to forsake their plan to conquer the Khazars and instead fight the Byzantines. The Arabs, however, managed to take Georgia from them.

What commenced the aggressive campaigns of the Khazars was the demise of the Western Turkish Khanate by a Chinese force. They no longer felt like vassals to another body, so they pursued a robust mission of expansion. Around 668 A.D. they had full control over the areas of the Black Sea and the Caspian Sea.

Now the dominant power of the steppes, the Khazars felt ready to challenge the Arab Muslims once again, mostly to win Georgia back. Round two of the Arab-Khazar war took place between the years 722 and 737 A.D.

The war was a plethora of seesaw tussles. At times the Khazars would gain the victory. For instance, in 730 A.D., they occupied Armenia and Georgia, and the northwestern region of Iran. The following year, they forged as far south as Iraq's Mosul and Syria's Diyarbakir.

But the war was won by the Arabs in 737 A.D.; they were led by the caliph Merwan. Fortunately for the Khazars, however, they did not face the devastating aftermath of losing to the Arabs that other defeated forces had to face. This was because the Umayyad Caliphate was dying and the Arabian forces had to relinquish all missions of rebellion and return to their fortress. The most serious request the Arabs had for the Khazars was for the khagan (meaning Emperor) to convert to a Muslim. He did so but because of the lax treatment of the Arabs he remained a nominal Muslim; it is believed that he renounced his faith as early as 740 A.D.

Strangely enough, the religion the Khazars chose to adapt was Judaism. Although historians debate over the exact time their conversion took place, the years 740 and 800 A.D. are proposed. The Khazars wanted to forsake their paganism and adapt a rather modern religion; they had three options at the time: Christianity, Islam and Judaism. They obviously chose Judaism. It is believed that the Khazars might be the progenitors of today's eastern Jews.

The Khazars held a cosmopolitan and liberal view; they held a strategic commercial center that linked the Muslim Abbasid (at Baghdad) with the Baltic.

They were followed by the rule of Magyars, Petchenges and Vikings. The Khazar state endured until 965 A.D. when the Kievan Prince Sviatoslav I destroyed Sarkel, the second stronghold city of the kingdom.

Viking Russia

Between the periods of the late 8th century and the early 9th century the regions of Volga was intensively permeated by commercial explorers. The eastern Baltic region and its indigenous inhabitants, namely the Slavs and Finns, were continuously pestered by the Scandinavian people known as Varangians which plundered and exploited the area. The raiders found a wealth of products there: honey, wax, products of timber, amber and furs.

The same incursion came from the south, particularly from the Don, Dnieper region and the lower Volga, but not from the same tribes. It was North African and Iranian commercial associations in seek of the same products and slaves. The Khazar state is highly linked to the southern activities.

860 A.D.

Rurik Becomes Prince of Novogard

As the activities of the southern regions waned, in around 830 A.D., commerce in the North Volga continued to flourish. So much so that the Varangian merchants that use to run their commercial operation from Lake Onega and Lake Ladoga instituted a stronghold in the area (modern day Ryazan). And for this establishment they instated their first nominal ruler, thereby establishing the first state before Kiev.

The Varangians were clannish tribes that were led by princes. Rurik, one of these princes, is believed to be the progenitor of the Rurik Dynasty that ruled over regions of East Slav until 1598. In 862 A.D. he spearheaded a force of Varangians to the city of Novgorod by the Volkhov River and conquered it.

The Varangians carried out raiding expeditions all the way to Baghdad and Constantinople.

882 A.D.

Oleg Founded Kievan Rus

Rurik's successor Oleg extended the Varangian territory to the south and conquered the city of Kiev, located around the Dnepr River. During the 5th century Kiev had been a city of the Slavs.

Oleg's invasion of the city commenced the first institution of a united, dynastic state within the area. It came to be known as Kievan Rus (882-1283 A.D.).

Shortly after its founding, Kiev became the epicenter of commerce between Constantinople, Scandinavia and the steppes. From Greece came merchants with fruits, wine, clothes, and gold, The Slavs from Rus would emerge with honey, wax and furs and the Hungarians and Czechs brought horses and silver.

The empire flourished for the following three centuries.

980-1015

Vladimir I

It can be said that the history of Kevan Rus truly began with Prince Sviatoslav. His interceding role in the 968-971 A.D. disputes of Byzantine-Danube Bulgar, his triumphant crusades against the Khazars, Volga Bulgars and other centers of Varangians—all this paved the way for the unification of his Rus clan.

His successor Vladimir I (980-1015) further fortified the state. He structured a political system of dynastic seniority under which the scattered colonies of the Rus were to be governed. Vladimir—by either annexing or destroying the scattered Varangian rule—expanded Kiev's territory. The kingdom's dominion stretched over upper Volga, Dnieper, Don, Neman, Dniester, and the western regions of Dvina.

988 A.D.

Vladimir I Adapts Greek Orthodoxy

Vladimir I led a life of debauchery; the chronicles maintain that he had about 800 concubines. His pagan life, however, stopped suiting him, so in 988 A.D., he sent a group of his envoys to solicit the best religion to adapt.

The envoy came back with an array of available religions and Vladimir chose Greek Orthodoxy, thereby creating an alliance with the West and Constantinople.

In 989 A.D., the subjects of Vladimir and his family were forced to accept the religion; this includes the Novgorod inhabitants. From Constantinople he had a bishop and a see established in Kievan Rus.

Medieval Russia

Medieval Russia was a tumultuous one that saw the fall of Kiev, the invasion of Mongol (Tatar rule), the rise of Moscow, the reincarnation of Rus rule and the foundation of a Russian state.

11th Century

The Erosion of Kievan Rus

The Rurik dynasty enjoyed decades of prosperity. Yaroslav the Wise succeeded Vladimir I; he brought Kievan Rus to its peak. Yaroslav made astute decisions that secured the development of the kingdom. He made wise alliances with bordering states, codified laws and supported the arts.

Yaroslav, however, did not make smart decisions in the end. He chose to divide his territories amongst his offspring who he believed would work as a unit to secure the longevity of the kingdom. He was very wrong. His children engaged in a lot of intra-fights and within a few decades of his death (1054), the kingdom was fragmented into regional powers. The semi-dominant forces were Novgorod of the northern region; Vladimir-

Suzdal of the north-eastern region; Halych-Volhynia, of the south-western region.

The survival of Kiev depended on two things: a united Rurik clan and a prosperous southern trade. Both of which began to degenerate in the late 11th century. What became the decisive factor of Kiev's doom was the invasion of the Mongol Golden Horde.

1223-1240

The Invasion of the Mongols (Tatar Rule)

The southern princes of Kiev Rus were bombarded by a surprise attack of the Mongols (commonly known as the Golden Horde or the Tatars). Within the span of a year (1237-1238), the Mongols managed to rule over large parts of Russia. They incinerated the northeastern cities, including Vladimir, ousted the Russians at the Sit River, and conquered Hungary and Poland in the west.

For the following years, the Mongols destroyed the chief cities of Kievan Rus, save Pskov and Novgorod. Although the regional princes were not overthrown, they were obliged to send various tributes to the Empire of the Golden Horde (the stronghold of the Mongol state). The Mongols also subjected them to a very extortionate tax imposition.

1283

The Emergence of Muscovy

It was the son of Alexander Nevsky (a Novgorod prince), Daniil Aleksandrovich, that established Muscovy or Moscow. The city first started out as an offshoot of Vladimir.

Muscovy's rise to prominence was facilitated by its princes who worked together with the Mongolian overlords. So close were they to the invaders that they were granted the right to collect tribute and taxes from other Russian principalities on their behalf. The rulers were titled the "Grand Prince of Moscow" by the Mongols.

Further enforcing the prominence of Muscovy was the establishment of the Russian Orthodox Church.

Ivan III Vasilyevich (Ivan the Great)

The princes of Moscow never wanted to remain lackeys of the Mongols forever. And the declining influence of the invaders in the middle of the 14th century became the first window of opportunity for a strike. In 1830, the Muscovite ruler, Dmitry Donskoy led a successful raid on the Mongols. He trounced the Mongol forces at the Don River at Kulikovo. Though he earned immense fame for his intrepid feat, the Mongols returned in strength two years later to reinstate Tatar rule in Muscovy. Things were to remain this way until the following century.

It took Ivan III or Ivan the Great (1462-1505) to do away with Tatar rule in Muscovy. He had a big vision for Moscow; following the collapse of Constantinople and the emperor who was the last Greek Orthodox Christian, he wanted Muscovy to become the 'New Rome.'

Ivan III had subverted other competing regional powers to extend his territory threefold; he annexed Tver and Novgorod. Now with a larger territory and a larger force, he felt ready to challenge the

Tatar rule. In 1480, he declared absolute rule over the nobles and princes of Russia and ripped the charter that made him liable to the tributes given to Tatar rule. The decaying and disintegrated Golden Horde attempted to crush the rebellion, but it lost the battle.

Ivan III came to be known as the 'Grand Prince of all Rus' and the 'Grandfather of all Russian Lands.' He structured the foundation for the emergence of a Russian state.

1478

Ivan Destroys Novgorod

It was during his expedition of expanding his territory that Ivan III came into conflict with Novgorod which had attempted to create an alliance with Lithuania. This act was seen a deviation from orthodoxy, or rather a reason of invasion, by Ivan.

Both regions entered a war in 1471 in which the Novgorod forces were defeated. Ivan imposed a war indemnity of 15,500 roubles and confiscated a large part of their northern provinces. The Novgorods also agreed to forsake any alliances with Lithuania.

But his rule in Novgorod was not without challenges for the people resisted his presence. In 1477, following his insistence to be recognized as sovereign (Gosudar), the Novgorods rejected his self-imposition on the land. He responded by putting the whole city under siege. His Moscow army encircled the city's chief monasteries until the signing of a treaty on 15th January, 1478 that recognized Ivan's rule over Novgorod by Archbishop Feofil of Novgorod (1470-1480).

The resistance of the people continued, but Ivan managed to crush each and every one of them.

Russia's Tsars

The Russian tsars were emperors of Russia who ruled before 1917. Several important events took place during the reign of Russia's Tsars.

1547

Ivan IV (Ivan the Terrible) Becomes the First Tsar

In 1547, Ivan IV (also called Ivan the Terrible) ascended to the throne and was entitled the first Tsar. The sixteen year old Tsar's reign commenced with constructive and continuous reformations, which were achieved due to the help he obtained from a clutch of boyars. By mid-16th century, the native administration was restructured, the military was reformed and a new law code was announced by Ivan IV.

Ivan the Terrible's leadership was austere and saw immense violence. He also suffered from depression and paranoia.

Livonian War

The region of Livonia was invaded by Ivan the Terrible in 1558. The war was instigated in hopes of securing a spot on the Baltic Sea. This twenty-five year long war initially was a success for Ivan; however, Russia had to burden nothing but problems.

The war involved Denmark, Sweden and the Polish-Lithuanian Commonwealth against Russia.

There was at last a peace agreement signed with Poland (in 1582) and Sweden (in 1583). All gains made initially in Livonia were ceded by Ivan IV. The regions on the Gulf of Finland, which belonged to Russia, were also relinquished to Sweden.

Ivan underwent some family problems in 1581 just before the war was concluded. During an argument he was having with his family, he beat his eldest and favorite son (also named Ivan and a potential heir). His grave injuries led to his death. Ivan's successor thus became Fedor I, his other younger son who was inadequate mentally.

Boris Godunov Becomes a Boyar

Ivan IV assigned two regents knowing that Fedor I was mentally deficient. Boris Godunov was one of the regents. In 1580, he assumed the rank of a boyar, when his sister was selected by Ivan to be Fedor's wife.

Around the year that Ivan IV died (1584), he had a newly born infant named Dmitry. This infant had support, but Boris Godunov didn't like it as he found the child intimidating. He therefore had the child and his mother sent away to Uglich. This destination is where Dmitry died in 1591, at just the age of 7. Boris is often linked to Dmitry's abbreviated life, even though evidence is scarce regarding this situation.

Boris confidently ruled during the reign of Fedor I— feeling as though he was the tsar himself. But this concept turned out to be a reality in 1598 following the death of Fedor, who died without having any children. The land assembly elected Boris to be a tsar.

The Three False Dmitry's

A nobleman of Russia journeys to Poland to spread the word that he was the son of Ivan the Terrible, Dmitry. He declared that he was the lawful successor to Moscow's throne. This pretender managed to persuade virtually everyone and headed to Russia together with his forces.

This nobleman's luck augmented when Boris unexpectedly died in 1605 and his wife and son were murdered two months later.

The self-proclaimed tsar's (Dmitry's) attempt to convince the grandees of Moscow failed and his foreign entourages were enraged. The false Dmitry was murdered in 1606 in Kremlin.

There was an emergence of a second Dmitry in 1607. Several people were reluctant to believe the second false Dmitry; this nevertheless didn't prohibit many from joining his movement. In 1607, he almost reached Moscow with an army of Cossacks, disgruntled Russians and Poles. He was later assassinated in the latter months of 1610.

The third false Dmitry emerged in 1612. Unlike the other two Dmitrys, the third one was apprehended and put to death within months of his arrival.

The history of Russia records the period from 1610 to 1613 as the "Time of Troubles" as it saw a time of incessant chaos.

1682-1725

Peter the Great Becomes a Tsar

Peter I was the son of the tsar, Alexis, by his second wife Natalia Naryshkina. Alexis' children from his first wife included his daughter, Sophia and sons, Fedor IIII and Ivan V. Both the sons were unable to rule, for the youngest child Ivan V, was deficient mentally and the eldest, Fedor, died when he was twenty years old, in 1682.

Ivan's inaptness to rule made the councils in Moscow declare Peter tsar. Sophia, however, was unhappy about the decision. She engineered a rebellion group composed of household troops (the Streltsy) which were disgruntled, against the family of Peter's mother (the Naryshkin).

They reached a resolution, with Sophia acting as regent and making Peter I and Ivan V joint leaders. Peter, at the age of ten, with his mother, was sent to live in Preobrazhenskoye's village by Sophia.

When Peter turned seventeen years old in 1689, Sophia feared she would no longer be a regent. She therefore devised a new plan to get rid of the Naryshkin clan together with the young tsar, but the plan was thwarted by the Naryshkin this time.

Peter finally ascended to the throne, firstly as co-tsar, until the death of Ivan V, his half-brother, in 1696.

Massive Transformation under the Rule of Peter I

During his reign, Peter made rapid transformations. He created new structures for the administration at central and local levels, he also got the fly-by-night army replaced with properly trained forces, and he introduced a navy of warships and a marine service.

Peter's reign also saw the launching of industrial enterprises. These enterprises amounted to as many as two hundred and they were mainly established for the building of weaponry and equipment for Peter's fleet and army, and the development of mines.

Education was also important in Peter's perspective, as it was highly encouraged during his reign. Schools that were secular were founded, where several texts from the west were translated into Russian. Russian students were sent abroad to study. The gentry's houses were visited by mathematics professors to teach their sons—for without attaining some educational background, marriage was prohibited.

In 1703, the first newspaper of Russia "Vedomosti, Records" was published.

Russia's currency and script was also reformed. The date of Russian New Year was changed to the 1st of January (previously 1st of September— supposedly the day the world was created).

Tackling corruption was also amongst his reformations.

Tsarevich Alexis Flees Russia

Peter I and his son Alexis were quite the opposite in many things. Alexis was prompted to flee Russia because of the tension between him and his father in 1716. He sought refuge with the emperor of Austria.

What Alexis did, in his father's view, was an act of treason. Thus, Peter the Great fools Alexis to come back to Russia with a tone of forgiveness. But all he did upon Alexis' return was incarcerate him and torture his mistress and his friends, all to find out proof of conspiracy.

Contrary to Peter's expectations, what he discovered was precious little. Alexis stated that he would shrink the navy's size and that he will return the capital to Moscow when he became tsar.

Alexis died in the fortress of St Petersburg after being whipped to the point of death with the dreadful "Knout" (the Russian whip). Alexis, three years prior, had a son, Peter II. ☒

Seventy Years of Empresses

This was indeed a remarkable era. Russia was under the rule of women for over seven decades, following the death of Peter the Great.

There were, of course, male emperors in between; but their astonishingly short time of rule didn't give them much importance in contrast to the four female emperors, who, in total, ruled for seventy-two years.

1724

Catherine I Becomes Empress

Catherine was a Lithuanian peasant when she first met with her future husband, Peter the Great, in early 1703. She was captured during the Northern War and used to work for a prince of Russia as a domestic serf. It was later in that year that Peter and Catherine had their first child and the church of Russian Orthodox received her.

Catherine and Peter overall had twelve children, with only two daughters surviving, Elizabeth (Yelizaveta) and Anna. Peter was first married to Eudoxia Lopukhina, then he divorced her and formally married Catherine in 1712. (It is believed that, in 1707, they were married in secret.) Catherine, in 1724, was crowned officially as empress.

Peter the Great died in less than a year and she became Empress Catherine I— the first woman to rule Russia.

Catherine I was uneducated, but it did not, in any way, truncate her strong character and commonsense which was an essential component to be a leader.

During her reign, she reduced the number of armies of Russia, which was around 140,000 (100,000 being Cossacks), as she found the military expenses deleterious to Russia's economy and it was not that necessary as Russia was also at peace. The military expenditure accounted for 65% of the annual revenue. Catherine I's advisors had control over many decision making in the country, but she, in this particular case, took a strong stand.

Her years as Empress, unfortunately, were rather short, as it only lasted for two years due to her death in 1727.

After Catherine's rule, the grandson of Peter the Great, Peter II, ascended to the throne at the age of twelve. He nevertheless died shortly after three years.

1730

Anna Builds a Court Composed of Foreigners and Upsets Russians

Anna was the daughter of Peter I's mentally-deficient half-brother Ivan V. Anna was raised mainly by her very strict mother, Praskovia Saltykova.

German, French, text of religion and folklore were a part of the education she received. Anna always liked a sumptuous society.

The Supreme Privy Council of Russia, following Peter II's death, decided to enthrone Anna. She became empress in 1730. Upon her ascension, she was required to sign "Conditions" by the counsel. These conditions stated that it was according to their counsel that she would rule and she was not at liberty to neither commence war nor call for peace without their permission. Their consent was also necessary for naming high officials and creating new taxes.

Anna was also forbidden to endow villages or estates, give promotion to people either from Russia or a foreign state, have the leeway to take punitive measures on nobilities without trial and use the state's revenue. Anna's circumscription of power ended when people (a separate party) took a stand against the creators of the counsel, Prince Galitzin and Dolgorouki. Anna assumed the monocracy following a petition that was conducted and made some of the constitution's creators flee to Siberia.

Anna's reign induced much indignation locally. This was mainly because she gave more room to foreigners. Her courts were virtually entirely filled with exotics--- the preponderance of them being Germans. The Germans were at liberty to make important decisions and were, in Anna's cabinet, given ruling positions. It is usually considered that this is due to Anna's lack of trust in the people of Russia. Many Russians therefore resented the Germans. The reign of Anna is even deliberately isolated from the history of Russia by historians all thanks to the enduring hate towards the Germans.

The lover of Anna was also a German named Ernest Johann Biron (hence her reign being referred to as "The Age of Biron").

According to historians, besides having leverage on foreign and domestic policies, Biron ruled at times.

In 1740, Anna died aged 47, after suffering from an extremely excruciating kidney disease which slowly brought her to her death.

Anna, upon her deteriorating health, declared that Ivan VI, her grandnephew who was just a one year old baby, should be her successor. Brion was also appointed regent by her. Anna was endeavoring to maintain her father's line—excluding the ascension of Peter the Great's descendants.

1741

Elizabeth Organizes a Coup

Daughter of Catherine I and Peter the Great, and cousin of Anna, Elizabeth organized a coup d'état to take over the Russian throne in 1741.

This successful feat was possible due to the support she obtained from the Russian regiments, who she was so kind to in the past. (She was also driven to this action due to Russian court members and French ambassador's influence, as they desired for the German control over the affairs of Russia to recede.) Elizabeth, on the 25th of November, 1741, got control over the throne of Russia with the aid of Preobrazhensky Regiment.

She arrested the infant emperor Ivan VI and his mother.

Elizabeth was crowned empress after summoning all the church and civil nobles of St. Petersburg. She vigorously restored Russia's interests and also her father's energetic mood.

Before Elizabeth died in 1762, she declared her nephew, Peter III, her successor.

Peter III assumed the throne early in 1762, but he was inadequate as a leader. He was rebellious, neurotic and a dedicated worshipper of Frederick II— Emperor Elizabeth's foe. His wife, who was a German princess, took his position in six months and took it with her for thirty-four years. Peter III was assassinated before the end of the year— it is often believed that his wife— Catherine the Great— was involved.

Catherine the Great Becomes Empress

The fervent and brilliant Catherine the Great became empress in 1762. In 1764 Catherine was successful in making education available for girls in Russia.

Before Catherine was crowned empress, she was in support of emancipating the serfs of Russia. An Instruction sketching a plan of reform was written by Catherine the Great, in 1767. This outlined plan was so radical that France prohibited its publication. The elected assembly was called upon to consider it. Shortly, it became obvious that the aristocracy was going to decline any reforms. Catherine shelved her plans as she needed their support.

Around the end of Catherine's rule, she stated that twenty-nine provinces were restructured, a lot of projects were subsidized, over one hundred towns were established and older ones were revamped or expanded. During her reign, there was an expansion of trade and development of communications.

Catherine died unexpectedly at the age of sixty-seven from a stroke.

The Early 19th Century Russia

The 19th century in Russia saw many historical events, ranging from Napoleon's attempt to invade Russia to Russia selling Alaska to America. It is also the era where one of the most memorable wars took place— the Crimean War.

1801

Alexander I Become a Tsar

Alexander I was Empress Catherine the Great's grandson— a grandson she wanted so badly to be her heir. She did not want her own son Paul I (Pavel Petrovich), father of Alexander I, to assume the throne. This is because Paul I's lack of stability deterred her highly; therefore she was resolute in disinheriting him.

The encyclopaedist, Denis Diderot, received an invitation from Catherine II to become the private tutor of Alexander I. After him, she summoned the Swiss citizen Frédéric-César La Harpe to become Alexander's instructor. He was a phenomenal teacher, who had lasting effect on Alexander's thinking.

Catherine the Great prepared a manifesto which denied the right of her son and selected her grandson to be the inheritor of the throne. Her abrupt death happened before appointing her grandson as her successor. Even though Alexander knew everything about the manifesto he chose to keep quiet, making his father Paul I emperor.

During Paul's reign, Russia was undergoing a dark period. His autocratic and peculiar deeds played to his disadvantage, as some military and noble men conspired against him. He was murdered in 1801; Alexander, the following day, became tsar.

Alexander righted the many wrongs of the previous reign. He made drastic improvements in his administration and jumpstarted a massive project for public education, which included the establishment of several schools.

Napoleon Invades Russia

The French ruler Napoleon Bonaparte, in 1799, ascended to power. He managed to annex large areas of European states including Germany, Italy, Croatia, Holland and Belgium—with the exception of Great Britain. He had allies from Russia, Prussia, Austria and Spain mostly because they were browbeaten into becoming one.

The relationship between Tsar Alexander I and Napoleon declined in 1810. In hope of punishing Great Britain, Napoleon created an embargo (called Continental System) in 1806, all to halt the British from trading with Europe. Alexander, owing to the negative impact it had on Russian trade, refused to act in accordance with Napoleon's plan. In addition, the tsar put a heavy levy on products of luxury from France and refused to allow Napoleon from marrying one of his sisters.

Since France didn't have any conflict with Russia in terms of territories, Napoleon believed that they were natural partners. But the infuriated Napoleon wanted to punish the tsar to teach him a lesson.

So in 1812, with a Grand Army totaling 600,000, Napoleon invaded Russia. Though Napoleon's army, which was by far the largest assembled force at that time, saw initial success, in six months, the Grand Army was almost completely annihilated. The factors which contributed to the Grande Army's disastrous failure was: freezing temperatures, disease, scarcities of food and Russian attacks.

Russia was backed by Prussia, Sweden, Austria and Great Britain. Then, in October 1813, Napoleon saw his defeat at the Battle of Leipzig. The Allies captured Paris in March, 1814, compelling Napoleon to exile to Elba.

1825

Nicholas I

Nicholas I was the brother of Alexander I. Nicholas wasn't raised to become Emperor and the chances of him becoming one were very slim.

Alexander I died unexpectedly in 1825. Constantine, Paul's second son, renounced the throne as he was wedded to a woman from Poland who was not of Royal descent. This made Nicholas the heir.

Nicholas grew up in a strict environment where flogging was conventional. He traveled to Britain and across Russia to complete his education.

1853-1856

The Crimean War

Nicholas's reign ended disastrously when he instigated the Crimean War in 1853 while attempting to seize the Ottoman Empire.

The conflict, which lasted for three years, was between the allies Britain, Turkey and France against the overpowered Russia. It was during this period that Russia realized it was incapable of competing with several powers from the west owing to its retrograde economy. Russia's massive military loss was a shock to Nicholas I.

Nicholas' health deteriorated and, in 1855, he died after catching the flu.

1867

Russia Sells Alaska to America

The deterioration of Russia's endeavors to expand settlements and trade was evident when Alaska was purchased in 1867.

In the 18th century, Russia showed great interest in Alaska, which had very few inhabitants and was abundant in natural resources. But due to lack of finance, Russia wasn't able to create large military presence and establish settlements in that region—the settlers of Russia didn't even amount to five hundred in Alaska. St. Petersburg even lost further interest when it was defeated in the Crimean War.

In 1867, Russia sold Alaska to America for $7.2 million. This marked the end of the presence of Russia in North America.

The Revolutionary Era of Russia

The late 19th century was a period of tumultuous and formative revolutions that gave the base to the formation of modern day Russia. It was the time when the sanguinary events of the Russo-Japanese war, Bloody Sunday and others took place.

The New Tsar Nicholas II

Following the death of his father, Alexander III, Nicholas II acceded to the throne. Nicholas II wasn't much of a feared or a revered leader in Russia. He sustained the policies and principles his predecessors believed in and almost every member in his government was a reactionary.

During his reign, Russia saw the greatest revolutionary movements; dissention reached its peak, supreme power fell in the hands of the people, even the Tsar era in Russia came to an end. But it wasn't his leadership that provoked these drastic changes. Of course his reluctance, terrible decisions and autocracy had a role to play, but the gradual yet drastic eruptions had much to do with the decade's long grievance the society bore.

1898

The Establishment of the Russian Social Democratic Labor Party

In 1898 there rose a socialist political party called "The Russian Social Democratic Labor", RSDLP ("Rossiyskaya sotsial-demokraticheskaya rabochaya partiya" in Russian). It was established by a group of Marxists in Minsk and it was purposed to unite the diverse parties in the Russian Empire and also give rise to the working class. The political structure of the RSDLP was based on the theories and ideologies of Friedrich Engels and Karl Marx.

The party was in favor of revolutions that revolved around economic, social and political matters. And the majority of its sympathizers were the intellects who upheld a rather radical view and the urban proletariat.

The powers-that-be in Russia weren't so fond of this revolutionary party; its members were treated with little or no tolerance. On March, 1898—following the conclusion of the First Congress— the Imperial Russian Police apprehended several representatives.

During this period the party was in a rather volatile state. But it started gaining some stability after Vladimir llyich Ulyanove (Vladimir Lenin) got on board.

In exile, the RSDLP held its Second Congress in Brussels five years later. The Second Congress was solely purposed to unify and cement the party, but before reaching any conclusion it was abruptly interrupted by the authorities in Belgium and they had to reschedule and relocate the congress to London.

On the 11th of August the congress met again in London and on the 17th of November they reached a decision that was to change the dynamics of the party for life.

The congress decided to divide the party in to two factions – the Bolsheviks (or Bolshinstvo in Russian, meaning "majority") and the Mensheviks (Menshinstvo in Russian, meaning "minority").

Julius Martov spearheaded the Mensheviks and Vladimir Lenin led the Bolsheviks. The argument that brought about this definitive split was the issue that revolved around the party's membership – who can claim it and its prerequisites.

Both wings issued their viewpoints and proposed their characterization of "party membership" before the congress.

"A member of the Russian Social-Democratic Labor Party is one who accepts its programme and who supports the Party both financially and by personal participation in one of the Party organizations," Lenin proposed.

"A member of the Russian Social-Democratic Labor Party is one who accepts the Party's programme, supports the Party financially, and renders it regular personal assistance under the direction of one of its organizations," Martov proposed.

Martov's proposal ended up winning more votes than that of Lenin's. And in respect of the party's platform, the Bolsheviks accepted their defeat and walked away in peace.

1904

War with Japan

The leaders of Russia had a rather insuppressible ambition to expand their territories to the Far East. And the construction of the Trans-Siberian Railroad was meant to facilitate this ambition with elements that would turn it in to a reality. Japan, on the other hand, was aware and completely opposed to the growing influence of Russia's power in the Far East.

And after the Sino-Japanese War in 1894-1895, in which China granted the occupation of the Liaodong Peninsula to Russia and

Taiwan to Japan, suspicion reached its peak and war began to loom.

During this period of war, a Japanese envoy made his way to the Gyeongbokgung palace and murdered the Korean Queen, Min. The mourning King Gojong then sought refuge in Russia and on his return declared his allegiance with Russia. This incident appalled the Korean society; it incited hate and indignation and it wasn't long before Japan completely lost all her influence in Korea.

Russia capitalized on this occurrence and built the Port Arthur (otherwise known as Lü-shun) at Liaodong Peninsula. After the construction of this fortress came to a completion, Russia brought in the "Russian Pacific Fleet" and asserted her defense for her occupation.

This hurled Japan in to full rage. And to make matters worse, Russia, in attempt to fortify her presence in the Far East, began to build the South Manchurian Railroad, and several inroads that lead into Korea.

For Japan this became an issue that only war can solve. However, several attempts were made to settle the matter through negotiation, but Nicholas II and his advisors failed to handle this negotiation properly.

"The Japanese government have at all times during the progress of the negotiations made it a special point to give prompt answers to all propositions of the Russian government. The negotiations have now been pending for no less than four months, and they have not yet reached a stage where the final issue can with certainty be predicted. In these circumstances the Japanese government cannot but regard with grave concern the situation for which the delays in negotiations are largely responsible."

-A telegram sent by Komura, Japanese foreign affairs minister.

On February 8th 1904, Japan declared war on Russia. Prior to the official declaration, however, Japan carried out an ambush on the Russian Pacific Fleet at Port Arthur.

Conclusion of the Russo-Japanese War

The Russo-Japanese War was a brief, yet a rather bloody one. The casualties of the war were incredibly heavy, with over 70,000 Japanese and 85,000 Russian lives lost.

Several battles were conducted during this period; Battle of the Yellow Sea, Battle of Yalu River, Battle of Mukden, Battle of Sandepu and so forth. Japan came out the victor in most of these battles.

The last conflict of the war was the Battle of Tsushima. To help the Russian troops at Port Arthur, the Russian Baltic Fleet (otherwise known as The Russian Second Pacific Squadron), which was under the command of Admiral Rozhestvensky, began sail. But while they were on their way, they hear reports of the demolishing of Port Arthur.

Admiral Rozhestvensky then decided to move on to Plan B and reach the harbor of Vladivostok. But the passage through which this seaport was to be reached was the Tsushima Straits, which laid in between Japan and Korea.

The commander knew the risks but decided to go for it either ways. The Baltic Fleet began sail through the Tsushima Straits at night. But then a Japanese scouting cruiser spotted the Russian fleet and contacted Admiral Tōgō Heihachirō.

The Japanese were prepared for such a move. And so when the signal came in, the Japanese rushed to combat the Russians. On the 27th and 28th of May, 1905 the battle on the Tsushima Straits commenced.

The Japanese completely destroyed the Baltic Fleet, with Russia loosing over 5,000 men while Japan lost just about 116 soldiers.

The war came to an official conclusion after the signing of the Treaty of Portsmouth on September 5th, 1905. It was arbitrated by Theodore Roosevelt, the American President.

1905

Bloody Sunday

"Bloody Sunday" is a name given to one of the most devastating days in Russia. On January 9th, 1905 Father Georgy Gapon, a priest that was also the head of the "Assembly of Russian Factory

Workers," amassed a crowd of about 150,000 and marshaled them to the Winter Palace in St Petersburg.

The crowd convened in the various churches in the city before the procession began. Knowing of this demonstration, the government arranged a force of about 120,000 men to stop the movement.

On Sunday morning, when the procession began, the armed forces managed to scatter a great portion of the crowd, mainly with the employment of incredible brutality. But still about 60,000 people managed to reach the gates of the Winter Palace.

The march was set out to be a peaceful demonstration, one that was purposed to simply present an appeal of humble demand to the Tsar, Nicholas II. But they were welcomed with extreme brutality and violence. The armed forces opened fire on the assembled crowd and ended up killing nearly 200 people and injuring over 800 people.

A scene from the July Days, the army has just opened fire on street protesters, by Viktor Bulla (1905)

Bloody Sunday left an indelible mark on the Russian society—a national scar that will be remembered by the generations to come—but it was also an incident that triggered a revolution that was to forever change the mechanism of Russia.

1905

The Signing of the October Manifesto

Bloody Sunday was an incident that triggered indignation throughout the whole of Russia. And not long after this bloodshed was the nation inundated by upheavals from everywhere and every class and group in the country. Workers went on several strikes, students demonstrated, the peasants organized insurgencies and much besides. There were even grievances and conflicts in the navy and army as well.

But in October, 1905 these upheavals reached their peak. In St Petersburg the workers established a constitutional body called the "Soviets of Workers' Deputies" (Soviet means Council).

Then on October, these workers organized a heavy demonstration, demanding the development of a democratic republic, (a Soviet in St Petersburg).

Emperor Nicholas II wasn't keen to consent these demands. The establishment of an elected legislative body was no principle that an autocrat can accept. But the counsel of Sergei Witte convinced the Tsar and on October 17th, Nicholas, with great reluctance, signed the October Manifesto.

The October Manifesto allowed the establishment of an elected legislator (or Duma in Russian). The proposal also stated that without the approval of the Duma no law was to be enforced.

Early 20th Century Russia

The 20th century was by far the most eventful era in Russia's history. It was the period that saw the launch of one of the world's epic battles in Europe; one that ushered in Russia's telling revolutions –upheavals that could not be altered or suppressed. It was a time that marked the end of the Tsar era and the birth of a new constitutional platform. So eventful, indeed it was.

1914

Russia in World War I

Russia's involvement in World War I had much to do with a treaty than anything else. As a matter of fact, if neutrality was possible, Russia wouldn't have scrupled from taking it.

Both militarily and economically weakened by the Russo-Japanese War and sporadic internal upheavals, Russia was not ready for this major conflict. But revoking the treaty Russia signed with Serbia and submitting to German's and Austria's demands would further degrade Russia's presence as a European power. And so Russia declared allegiance with Serbia and entered the war.

Though poorly accoutered and organized, the Russian soldiers fought with great zeal and triumphed on most occasions. The army's performance in WWI helped ignite a nationalistic feeling in the country. But Tsar Nicholas II failed to make use of this national sentiment. As a matter of fact he made decisions that were not only detrimental to the nation but also to the monarch itself.

Alongside the advancement of the war, Russia's internal problems began to exacerbate. Funding the war instigated inflation; food shortage reached its peak, the suffering of peasants increased tremendously, grievance, in general, was dwelling in the homes of every one in Russia. And to make matters worse, Nicholas II used his arbitrary power to dismiss the reformation proposals issued by the State Council and Duma – the Progressive Bloc being one of them.

1917

The February Revolution
The rippling effects of World War I on Russia and Nicholas' reluctance and autocracy lead to the eruption of what is known as one of Russia's greatest revolutions "The February Revolution."

The February Revolution otherwise known as "Russian Revolution of 1917" was the grand event that brought the Tsar era to an end and changed the political mechanism of Russia.

"The February 1917 revolution grew out of prewar political and economic instability, technological backwardness, and fundamental social divisions, coupled with gross mismanagement of the war effort, continuing military defeats, domestic economic dislocation, and outrageous scandals surrounding the monarchy," Rabinowitch explains the cause of the February Revolution.

On February 23rd 1917, which was also "International Women's Day," a throng of women flocked the streets of the capital in demonstration for equal rights. This crowd was then unexpectedly fastened together by women who worked in the textile industry. The latter were there to voice their grievance over the massive shortage of bread.

This crowd then gradually began to grow, with other women and men workers now at the forefront. The march persisted for days. Alarmed by the growing rate of this demonstration, the powers-that-be then commanded the armed forces to dissolve the mass by way of any means necessary – open fire included.

But when the soldiers reached the crowd, they had an about-face and they decided to join the campaigners instead.

This twist of events eventuated in the February Revolution and the fall of the Romanov Dynasty.

1917

The End of the Tsar Era

The February Revolution led to the conclusion of the Tsar era. The society's relationship with the monarch was already at a low ebb when the workers and soldiers joined forces.

On 2nd of March, following the formation of the "Soviet of Workers and Soldiers Deputies", Nicholas II, left with no other choice, announced his resignation and passed the throne over to the Grand Duke, his brother Michael Alexandrovich.

Michael promptly declined the offer, and that refusal marked the end of the Tsar era.

1917

The October Revolution

The October Revolution was yet another major event that took place in the same year as that of the February Revolution.

After the fall of the monarch, Russia stood without a leader. And attempting to fill up this void and mitigate the nation's unrest, the Duma allowed the formation of a Provisional Government.

The Provisional Government, which was otherwise known as the Russian Republic, was initially headed by Prince Georgy Yevgenyevich Lvov. The new head of state promised the restoration of order in the nation and amendment of the rights of workers. But the continuation of the war still kept on causing more economical problems for Russia, and the society had very little to alleviate its grievance.

In the coming months, Prince Lvov, was replaced by Alexander Kerensky. Kerensky did whatever was possible to gain full control over the country, but Russia's continual participation in the war, added to the worsening economic conditions, repelled a major part of its supporters.

Then nine months after the Russian monarch saw its down fall and the Provisional Government rose to power, there came a force to be reckoned with— the Bolshevik.

The Bolsheviks, with Lenin as their leader, managed to gather enough support from the populace. They promised to end Russia's partaking in the war and propagated their "peace, land and bread" program. Then on October 24th – 25th the party managed to organize a coup and oust the provisional government.

The council accepted the formation of the new government, which was mainly composed of Bolsheviks, after the October Revolution.

1918

The Civil War

The Bolsheviks rising to power had its moment of elation in Russia. But it wasn't long before it was faced with harsh and persistent oppositions.

The ruling party managed to end Russia's participation in World War I by way of signing the highly controversial Treaty of Brest-Litovsk in 1918. This treaty and other decisions of the party triggered quite a heavy revolt, especially from the White Russians and the peasants, on whom Lenin declared "ruthless war on the kulaks, death to all of them."

From that point on Russia became the hub of an incredibly brutal civil war. It last for about three years and thousands of people died during this time. At the end the Bolsheviks triumphed.

A year after the civil war came to an end, Russia was struck by yet another devastation – a famine that claimed the lives of about twenty million Russians.

Modern Russia

The establishment of the Soviet Union absolutely changed Russia's political dynamics. This union had its virtues and drawbacks, which in so many ways made Russia's history all the more interesting.

From the mid-20th century to present, quite a lot occurred in Russia. Russia's partaking in World War II, the Cold War, the collapse of the Soviet Union, the BRICS are but a few.

1922

The Formation of the Soviet Union

The Soviet Union or the Union of Soviet Socialist Republics came into formation on December, 1922.

The union was a conglomerate of several republics; the Russian SFSR, the Belarusian SSR, the Ukrainian SSR and the Trans-Caucasian SFSR. It was established by the Bolsheviks.

Then on July 6th 1923, the union was introduced to a new platform, one that resulted in the formation of the All Union Congress of Soviets.

1939-1945

The World War II

The rise of the National Socialist German Workers' (Nazi) party in Germany was a bugbear to the Soviet Union ever since 1933. This anxiety proved valid when Germany's lust for expansion to the east was pronounced after the signing of the Munich agreement on September 29, 1938—a settlement the Soviet Union stoutly opposed.

Despite the many wars the Soviet Union conducted after the start of WWII (in Poland and Finland), it was on June 22, 1941 that the official war between Germany and the USSR commenced. Spearheaded by Germany, the Axis forces marched across the borders of Russia, put Leningrad (now Saint Petersburg) under siege, captured Ukraine and made threats to capture Moscow.

The Red Army countered the German forces from Moscow and continued to undermine them. In the Kursk and Stalingrad battles the USSR trounced the German forces and tipped the balance in the favor of the Allies.

By 1944, Russia's borders had pushed further into Eastern Europe.

At the Yalta Conference the Soviet head Stalin, Churchill and Roosevelt met on February 1945 at Yalta to convene on Europe's territorial dissections and WWII's last phases.

1945-1990

The Cold War

Following a dispute between the U.S. president Harry Truman and Stalin in the Potsdam Conference in 1945 over matters of Eastern Europe, the former Yalta allies turned rock-ribbed enemies.

The two nations established two opposing blocs: the U.S instituted the North Atlantic Treaty Organization (NATO) and Russia, the Warsaw Pact.

For the following five decades the two nations were involved in a legion of political and economic warfare that never culminated to an actual war.

1991

The Soviet Union Collapses

In the 80s the Soviet Union was plagued by a collapsing economy, a decaying political structure and much besides. The power struggle between the then president Mikhail Gorbachev and the statesman, Boris Yeltsin (future president of Russia), also exacerbated the crumbling USSR.

Russia's economic struggle officially hit its peak when on December 1991 a system of food rationing was imposed on Saint Petersburg and Moscow. The situation culminated to a point where Russia was receiving foreign humanitarian food aid.

On December 25th 1991, the Soviet Union came to its official end, ushering in the rule of the Russian Soviet Federative Socialist Republic.

2009

Russia Becomes a Member of the BRICS

Brazil, Russia, India, China and South Africa, BRICS, was first instituted by four countries; it was in 2009 that South Africa joined the team.

Although the member states first met on September 2006 in New York City, their official summit took place on June 16th, 2009 in Yekaterinburg, Russia.

The team is composed of developing economic world powers. The GDP of the five nations accounts for about 20% of the gross world product. That's an estimate of about $16.039 trillion.

BRICS has held seven summits, two of which Russia has hosted. Russia is also the current chair holder of the group.

2014-2015

The Ukrainian Conflict and Russia's Annexation of Crimea

Following his exile after the 2014 Ukrainian Revolution, the president of Ukraine, Viktor Yanukovych, appealed to the Russian government to take military actions to restore Ukraine's political, economic and civil unrest. Russia's current president Vladimir Putin responded by dispatching Russian forces throughout Crimea and the south eastern regions of Ukraine.

Though deemed invalid by Western forces, the Crimean Status Referendum was held in which 93% of the electorate voted to separate from Ukraine and join Russia.

Russia repeatedly trespassed Ukraine's boarders thereby breaching the 1914 Budapest Memorandum.

The West imposed the first ever sanctions on Russia.

The conflict rose to the arm conflict of warring parties which claimed a considerable amount of lives and Russia annexed Crimea.

Printed in Great Britain
by Amazon